THE LIBERATED FATHER'S HANDBOOK

Written and Illustrated by Andy Myer

St. Martin's Press New York

ACKNOWLEDGMENTS

—*To David Lott, who has been a superb editor, agent, promoter, sounding board, general adviser, and friend. Thanks for letting me run with this ball.*

—*To my wife, Sandi, for her unshakable enthusiasm, her invaluable assistance, her uncommon common sense, her willingness to reread the same passage three times a day, and, above all, for giving me three exquisite daughters.*

Library of Congress Cataloging in Publication Data

Myer, Andy.
  The liberated father's handbook.

  1. Fathers.   I. Title.
HQ756.M86   1983   306.8′7   83-9674
ISBN 0-312-48350-3 (pbk.)

First Edition

10 9 8 7 6 5 4 3 2 1

To my three greatest joys: Stacy, Jessica, and Lindsay

Contents

Introduction

Fatherhood. The word still brings to mind images of mustachioed men reigning over ordered and obedient households. After a grueling day of oppressing hapless workers at the nearby shoe factory, Papa would strut up the front steps of his freshly painted three-story home to be greeted by a demure and cheerful wife. Young Bertram would bow, little Agatha would curtsy, and Baby Amelia, freshly powdered and bundled, would be brought in for a paternal kiss. This man would rather have been turned into a slug than change the baby's diaper.

Such patterns of behavior changed most appreciably in the late 1960s, when the baby boom generation* began to emerge from college. Millions of young people experimented with alternative lifestyles, engaged in promiscuous sex, smoked marijuana, engaged in more promiscuous sex, and ate lentil-walnut burgers. These changes, coupled with the rise of feminism in the late 1970s, have altered the way many young people approach parenthood.

This book is addressed to that product of change—the prospective father who is eager to shoulder his share of the responsibilities but is frankly confused by everything that follows conception. (There are a good many more who are equally be-

---

*The baby boom began the day after World War II ended. People were so happy and relieved, they had uninterrupted sex for the next fifteen years.

wildered about what *precedes* conception, but that information is covered extensively elsewhere.)

No single work could possibly hope to cover every aspect of gynecological visits, problems during pregnancy, natural childbirth, labor, postpartum complications, and finding babysitters. Yet, if by the last chapter these topics seem less ominous and perplexing, if the new father or father-to-be can approach his changed station in life with some measure of comfort and optimism, then this book will have achieved its goals.

1

Raw, Unadulterated, Torrid Sex

Intercourse

Anyone holding a book called *The Liberated Father's Handbook* is already well enough acquainted with the workings of the human body not to need them repeated here. Move on to the next chapter.

2

Guess Who's Coming to Dinner . . . and Breakfast . . . and Lunch

Confirming the Pregnancy

The decision to have a baby is a serious one, and should be preceded by a careful examination of your own and your wife's attitudes toward child-rearing, your financial status, and your willingness to sacrifice large amounts of time and effort to the raising of a new individual. More often, however, it is preceded by the discovery that someone forgot to pick something up at the drugstore.

Either way, you may come home for dinner one night and be told during a contented mouthful of macaroni creole that you are going to be a father. No matter how thorough your mental preparation has been for this moment, the news will undoubtedly bring to the surface many conflicting expectations, fears, and concerns. Hide them! Nothing is more irritating to a woman who has thrown up four times since breakfast than a spouse who suddenly develops cold feet. While everyone's response will vary, try to place yours somewhere between absolute ecstasy and "Hey, that's swell. . . . Pass the ketchup."

Confirmation by a doctor is essential, but most women don't get to see their gynecologist for several more weeks. This is an eternity for an anxious couple. Most opt to purchase one of the new, inexpensive pregnancy-testing kits available over the counter at any drugstore. The kit will give a fairly accurate result and is simple to use. A chemical sprayed inside the enclosed test tube reacts positively to an enzyme present in the urine of pregnant women. If a donut shape appears at the bottom of the vial after several hours, your wife is pregnant; if not, then you have an unusual bud vase for the kitchen table.

If the testing kit and subsequent doctor visit confirm that your wife is pregnant, then you are faced with the responsibilities of helping her through the remaining difficult months. Aside from the initial physical discomforts (notably morning sickness and tenderness of the breasts), your wife will probably have heightened psychological and emotional needs. She may experience sudden bouts of depression and uncontrollable weeping. She may be concerned that she is becoming "unattractive" or even "ugly." You should scrupulously avoid terms that might upset her, such as big, large, bulky, wide, vast—and most particularly "protuberance."

Your wife may also come under the influence of the phenomenon commonly referred to as "the nesting instinct." Consequently, you should try not to overreact if she attempts to line your bed with twigs, leaves, and bits of string.

Finally, many couples wonder if sex is possible during pregnancy. Theoretically it is, but it is very complicated and against the law in most states without first passing an approved course that includes a minimum of twenty-five hours of actual practice with an instructor present. In parts of Utah, sexual contact during these months is banned altogether, and any convicted couple is immediately taken to a detention center and forced to watch "CHiPs" reruns for three to five days, depending on the judge. Obviously, if you feel compelled to engage in this sort of distasteful activity, first contact your state department of health or county health commissioner's office.

3

No Man's Land

Going to the Gynecologist

As a conscientious father-to-be, nothing is more unnerving than accompanying your wife for her gynecological examinations. As you open the waiting room door, you are confronted with a dozen or so women, all of whom are about to have their most intimate recesses probed and prodded, probably by a man. You have intruded on a secret society. You have stumbled into the inner sanctum. You are not welcome here. It is best at this point to cough in an offhand way, casually sit down as though you had found an empty seat in a bus terminal, and become engrossed in the nearest copy of *American Fetus,* even if its only readable article is "Circumcision: Friend or Foe" by Dr. Lyle Tweedler.

Shortly after you arrive, your wife will be called into the office to be weighed (which will make her irritable) and to have a blood sample drawn (which will make her irritable and sore). She will return to the waiting room for another fifteen to sixty minutes, depending on the crowd size at the time.

At some point during the pregnancy you may decide to be present during the examination itself. This will afford you the opportunity to sit for another thirty to fifty minutes in a room far smaller than the one you've been in for the past hour. For the imaginative, there are some small diversions. Sit on the doctor's stool (the one with wheels) and spin around the room, executing pirouettes and figure-eights until you become nauseated. Don't

miss the series of plaster models showing the stages of embryonic development. Acquaint yourself with some of the instruments and equipment in the room. Reexamine the models of embryonic development.

Throughout all of this, try to be reassuring to your wife. Engage in small talk, as though there could be nothing more normal in the world than for you to be in the same room with her while some guy you've never met comes in and inserts three fingers into her vagina.

Your first moments with the doctor after he arrives are critical. This is when you should let him know in no uncertain terms what you expect from the childbirth experience in general and from him in particular. You might want to begin by stating that while he will have your complete cooperation, you and your wife are not about to be bullied into unnecessary treatments, or to allow yourselves to become mere cogs in the workings of an uncaring and arrogant medical establishment.

If you're smart, though, you'll just wave and say, "Hi!"

Don't hesitate to ask the doctor questions that may have occurred to you, no matter how silly or trivial you feel they may seem. This is also the chance to air any physical or psychological complaints that your wife may be experiencing. Most likely the doctor will say, "That's normal." Problems that are considered normal during pregnancy are nausea, back pain, depression, sore nipples, swollen breasts, diarrhea, irritability, swollen feet, tingling in the extremities, frequent urination, blurred vision, ringing in the ears, and UFO sightings at the deli counter of the supermarket.

After the examination has been completed, your only remaining task is to enter into a ten-minute negotiation with the receptionist to set up the next appointment. No matter how carefully this is done, in three or four weeks time, a day before the examination, you will realize that it coincides exactly with a round-robin racquetball tournament you had high hopes of winning.

Repeat this process about fourteen times during the pregnancy.

Belinda Wallace
Paul Edna
Alastair
Myrna Ellen JEFFERY
Everett AMY WILDA
Geoffery George Jason
Flora Jeanette INGRID
KELLEY JARED BETH
Rosalie Renee Olga
LYLE
Herbert
Marion MARIO
MELVILLE Etta
TOBY Vaughn
Tyrone Janet EVA
ANDREA TED
Ethel
THAD Glenda
FRANCINE EUNICE
BRIAN Elise INA
SAMUEL
JILL RACHEL Max FRITZ

4

A Rose by any Other Name . . .

Naming the Baby

Wife:	"How about the name 'Brian'?"
Husband:	"Naw. There was a Brian who used to sit behind me in homeroom and pick his nose."
Wife:	"Well, then how about 'Astrid' for a girl?"
Husband:	"What would they call her for short, 'Ass' or 'Trid'?"

Variations on this dialogue are repeated dozens of times during a typical pregnancy, and they can be a serious source of disagreement for the expecting couple. Assigning a name to an unformed individual is an inherently difficult task; compounding the problem are the following considerations:

1. *Family names or names in honor of someone.* If your name is James Allen Campbell III, then there may be some degree of family pressure in the event of a son. Similarly, if Grandpa Elmo has just cashed in all his chips, Grandma Edna may threaten to write you out of her will if you don't name your

child after him. Pray for a girl. Failing that, see if you can appease her with "Ellery." Good luck.

2. *Ethnic names.* Obviously, if your last name bears the stamp of a particular country or region, there will be large numbers of names that simply will not be appropriate. Examples of unsuitable combinations are Manuela Abramowitz, Guido O'Hanlon, and Anastasia Ming.

3. *Unpleasant associations.* Many historical names, such as Adolf, Benedict, Rasputin, Genghis, Attila, and Marie Antoinette, will probably be eliminated because of this phenomenon. Personal experiences also bias our judgment for or against names. Consider, for example, the following scenario: at your sixth birthday party, a kid named Seymour hid your pet goldfish behind a veal cutlet in the back of your mother's Whirlpool freezer. That would be a name you would certainly not consider for your child.*

*Who would want to name his baby "Whirlpool" anyway?

4. *Fads*. Names go in and out of fashion regularly, and any couple who wants to pick an original or unusual name should be aware of what's "going around." During the 1950s, "Dave," "Michael," "Barbara," and "Debby" were quite popular. More recently, biblical names have come into vogue, and the average nursery school class list reads like a "Who's Who" of Leviticus. Presently we are at the tail end of a "J" cycle, and you can't go to a playground without tripping over a "Jeremy," "Joshua," "Jennifer," or "Joanna."

5. *Good names*. "Stacy," "Jessica," and "Lindsay" (see Dedication).

5

The Jell-O Mold that Ate Lansing

Surviving the Baby Shower

The baby shower has changed radically in recent years. Women who used to be stuck going to these things by themselves are now dragging their husbands with them. If you must go, then by all means be aware of what you are in for.

Showers are usually held at the home of a friend or relative about a month before the baby is due. You should arrive about forty-five minutes after the party is called for, so that the guests, many of whom have never met each other before, have had a chance to engage in extremely strained conversation.

Once inside the front door (or side door if it's a "surprise" party), you are buffeted about the room like a dinghy in a gale, lost in a sea of relatives, friends, acquaintances, and utter strangers. Finally, dazed and exhausted, you find a sanctuary in the storm: the serving table.

Ah, the serving table. There is danger and disappointment lurking on top of every platter and inside every bowl. Do not approach this area without careful preparation and study (see diagram). On either side of the table (positions 1 and 9) are dishes bearing tiny crustless sandwiches filled with cream cheese and cucumber; next to Styrofoam packing peanuts, these are the least satisfying foodstuffs in the Western world. Behind them, on heated trays (positions 2 and 8), are bits of hot dog wrapped in biscuit dough, called "pigs in a blanket." These aren't bad, but care should be taken not to sustain second- and third-degree burns to your tongue and inner cheeks. The beverage (position 3) is most often a champagne punch with a dollop of sherbet drifting around the bowl like an iceberg looking for a freighter. This also is quite tasty, but only if you manage to shoulder your way to the front of the line so that you

can fish out the sherbet for yourself. There are usually plates of cheese, vegetables with dip, and potato chips (positions 4, 5, and 6), all of which can be ingested safely in any amount. In the middle of the table (position 7) is the *pièce de résistance,* the centerpiece, the main event. This is generally a fruit-flavored Jell-O that, to the untrained observer, seems to have a compost heap suspended inside it. It does. Swallow at your own risk.

The reason the food has been described at such length is to allow you to make your choices wisely and quickly. You and your wife may be allowed only a few moments at the serving table before being ushered into the living room for the ritual opening of the presents. This portion of the shower will require delicacy, sensitivity, diplomatic skill, and stamina.

Suppose, for example, that you have opened a package containing a yellow stretch suit* from your friend Val. You can't simply say, "Thanks, Val." No, you have to say something like, "Gee, Val, this is great! Look, Doreen! I guess these are purple giraffes across the top? They're ostriches? Hey, that's just great. God, they didn't have clothes like this when I was a kid, though I guess I just don't remember that well, heh heh. Well, gee, thanks again, Val, that's great. Just great. Here, pass it around . . ."

---

*A stretch suit is a one-piece outfit with a large array of snaps that allow for easy access to the baby's diaper without totally undressing the baby. There are many styles, all of which are designed to leave at least one unmatched snap hanging out at the end.

The stretch suit is then passed to the person nearest at hand, who pretends to scrutinize it as though it were actually the Rosetta Stone, examining the smallest detail of tailoring, reading the laundering instructions, then holding it out to get the overall effect and nodding in approval. The hapless rag is then handed to the next person, and the process is repeated until it has made its way back to the beginning.

Of course, even though you have thanked everyone profusely for the presents as you opened them, that is not enough. They all expect to be thanked again—in *writing*. This can be an extremely tedious and time-consuming task if you attempt to write personalized notes to each of the shower participants. Sanford Tiltz, a graduate student of graphology, has devised the following cryptogram to serve as a ready-made, all-purpose thank you note. All you have to do is fill in the name of the recipient and your signature.

Dear

Sincerely,

Remarkably, in one comprehensive follow-up study involving 500 shower participants, only one questioned the contents of the thank you and 115 sent replies thanking Tiltz for his thoughtful note. The sample can be easily reproduced at any local print shop for a nominal fee that is well worth the saved hours and uncramped hands.

6

"Hey, Mister! Have I Got a Crib for You!"

Preparing the Nursery

Every expectant couple eventually has to face the prospect of converting that "spare" room into a nursery. You know the room. The one containing your college textbooks, two tennis rackets with broken strings, a Jimi Hendrix poster, three forlorn boxes of record albums, and a crate crammed with the mauve plastic tableware you used to eat off of when you were a bachelor.

Once you have carted these priceless mementos off to their permanent burial places in the attic, garage, or basement, you can go to work on the room itself. If the walls still bear the bamboo-motif velour wallpaper from the previous owner, you may have to consider painting or recovering them. There are certainly no definitive rules to follow, but you should try to make the room bright without being harsh. Irreparable psychological damage may result from keeping a child in a dark brown or cadmium orange room. (A recently completed twenty-year study by Dr. M. O. Vashnagel of Yale University examined the effects of a maroon environment on children. There were large numbers of sexual deviants, criminals, prostitutes, runaways, and an unusually high percentage of life insurance salesmen.)

The largest expenditure will obviously be on furniture. Most dealers of baby furniture have "Uncle" in front of their names in the phone book. Don't be fooled. Treat these salesmen with the same disrespect and skepticism that you would bring to a used car dealer.

The most important item, of course, is the crib. It should be sturdy and safe. The bars should be close enough together to ensure that the baby's head cannot become wedged between them. One side should lower to allow for easy access to the baby. The mattress should be firm, and made of a hypoallergenic material. The bars of the crib come in numerous styles (see diagram). If you have trouble remembering all of this, write it down on a small piece of paper you can conceal in the palm of your hand.*

The assembly of the crib after it has been delivered is not difficult and should not require more than a half hour's work if you avoid three common mistakes. First, many people try to connect the auxiliary transmission cable linkage after the flywheel housing has been welded to the brake release coupler block. The cable should be connected first. Second, the transverse caliper sprocket jets are often reversed, causing the water pump bearings to seize up. The blue-colored hoses should be on top, the red-colored on the bottom. The third and most common error is the failure to let the guys from the furniture store set the damn thing up when they deliver it.

*You guessed it— a crib sheet.

Another essential item is a chest of drawers with a top that flips down to become a changing table. This is where you will most often diaper the baby. Changes of clothing and other often-used items should be stored in the second or third drawers, as it is virtually impossible to get into the top drawer with the baby on it. Should you, nevertheless, need to use that drawer during a changing, employ the following procedures:

1. Move the baby to the stationary portion of the table.
2. Holding the baby firmly with your left hand, lift the hinged portion of the table with your right hand and hold it up with your forehead.
3. With your right hand, open the drawer and extract the item.
4. Inadvertently drop the item on the floor.
5. Keeping your left hand in a protective position, quickly bend down and pick up the item.
6. Get smacked on the back of the head by the falling wooden flap of the changing table.
7. Regrasp the baby. If your eyesight is slightly blurred at the moment, simply follow the sound of your child's appreciative laughter.

If the furniture salesman will allow it, try this out with a number of models to see which one works best for you. If not, practice this at home before the baby arrives, substituting your neighbor's cat for the baby. The entire maneuver should take less than six seconds, not counting the application of Band-Aids.

The final mandatory purchase for the nursery is the diaper pail. You should make every effort to perfect your technique with this deceptively simple device. Strive to develop a smooth, assured swing that allows you to release the diaper at the precise moment the lid begins its descent. Properly executed, the pail should be open for only two seconds. Many first-time fathers who took a casual attitude toward diaper-pail timing have spent miserable, mortifying days smelling like the washroom in a bus depot.

7

Birthing 101

Childbirth Preparation Class

While women have been enduring childbirth for eons, for most of that time it was a pretty nasty business, what with all the screaming and chanting and people bringing leeches to suck out the bad humours. Not surprisingly, many women did not survive the ordeal. The advent of modern medicine brought many innovations, among them the sterile operating room, anesthesia, Richard Chamberlain, and no more leeches. However, the pregnant woman was still treated as though she were "sick," instead of being a perfectly healthy individual involved in a normal reproductive act. She would be ceremoniously carted off into the forbidding halls of the maternity ward, while her husband paced helplessly in a dingy, cramped, smoke-filled room, sharing one ten-year-old back issue of *Reader's Digest* with seven other guys who obviously hadn't had a chance to shower in several days. The laboring woman was invariably anesthetized as birth approached, so that when it was all over, neither husband nor wife had any recollection of one of the most important events in their lives. People paid good money for this.

Then in the 1940s a French obstetrician, Ferdinand Lamaze, promoted a technique that used breathing and relaxation to facilitate childbirth without the use of anesthesia. This grew rapidly in popularity with everyone (except the anesthesiologists), and today large numbers of expecting couples opt to try for a "natural" childbirth.

Lamaze classes, now more often referred to as "childbirth education" classes, are usually eight weeks in length. You will be asked to bring with you two pillows, a blanket, and a watch with a second hand. These are for a surprise parlor game that concludes every session and is too revolting to describe here. The classes are generally held at a nearby hospital, but depending on your community's available space and funds, it may take place in a local "Y" or barely heated church basement. If your sessions are held in a school or other teaching facility, the only seating available for your wife may be one of those student desks with the fixed writing table. Come a little early that first night, as it may take her five or ten minutes to figure out how to sit down.

Many couples spend a large portion of the initial class "checking out" the other couples; this is a perfectly human reaction to a new situation, so you should not feel ashamed if you find yourselves doing it. In fact, the sample descriptions below may help you characterize the participants in your own class.

1. *Who Let Them In?* They arrive in a canary yellow Porsche. The husband has a beeper on his belt, and appears to be an upwardly mobile corporate lawyer who makes more in a week than you do all year. His squash racquet is visible in the backseat of the car. The wife is undoubtedly a professor of nuclear astrophysics on leave of absence. Eight months pregnant, she looks like Cheryl Tiegs with a cushion tied around her waist. They carry goose-down pillows with Louis Vuitton pillowcases.

2. *Middle America.* They arrive in a lime-green Omni still bearing the remnants of a "Ford for President" bumper sticker. The husband is a button-down-collar type who probably works for a company that designs valve couplings for nuclear missiles. The wife is a pleasant-looking woman who closely resembles your next-door neighbor whom you haven't spoken to in over a year; now that you look closely, you realize it *is* your neighbor. Wave. She and her husband are carrying foam pillows in blue "Dreamspun" pillowcases by Fieldcrest.

3. *The Wheat Germ Set.* They hitchhike to the meeting. Obviously no one told them that the revolution is over. The husband is a solemn dude with a headband and a torn army
jacket emblazoned with the slogan "Free the Guy from North
Smithersville." The wife, a gaunt woman whose disheveled
hair has the color and texture of a week-old Brillo pad, is
licking brewer's yeast off her fingers. They have inflatable
pillows from Kasselman's Army/Navy store.

4. *Mr. and Mrs. Neanderthal.* They sputter into the parking lot
in a battered Chevette with unpainted body putty over the
left rear wheel well. The husband is wearing a knit cap with
shrapnel from beer cans woven into it; he seems dispropor-

tionately upset over missing the wrestling match on cable. His wife is in a green shift with a map of the Hawaiian Islands printed on it. It is impossible to see their pillows, which are concealed in a Korvettes bag.

Having completed this mini-survey, you will meet the nurse or specially trained childbirth instructor and begin the actual coursework. The first half of each class is devoted to instruction; principally, this covers the stages of labor and the breathing and relaxation techniques that have been developed to accomodate them. For example, in the early stages of labor, a shallow, rhythmical puffing may be sufficient. As the intensity of the contractions increases, the woman may have to switch to a complex series of gasps, snorts, whistles, hoots, and grunts that are best left to the instructor to describe. It would be wise to bear in mind that childbirth education personnel are usually seriously "into" birth, and probably have the placentas from their own children's births in Lucite cubes on conspicuous display in their own homes. This bias does tend to shade their descriptions of the delivery, so it might be advisable as you jot down notes to replace a phrase such as "considerable discomfort" with "extreme torment," or "adverse reaction" with "OhShitOhGodOhGodOHGODOHGODaaaaaAAA AARRRRRRGGGGGGGHHHHHHHHHHHHHH!!!!!"

After a short break, the entire group is then required to practice the material that has just been covered. The women all lie down on the floor. As the husband or coach, you will have to learn how to keep your wife as comfortable as possible, to help her focus her attention *away* from her pain, time her contractions, pace her

breathing, and how to be supportive at all times. So stop gazing at
the cute nuclear astrophysicist over there in the corner.

For many husbands, the worst moment of the evening comes
during the practice of the "Kegel" exercise (this should not be confused with a "kugel" exercise, which is performed with a noodle
casserole). Also referred to as the "elevator" exercise, it is intended
to strengthen the muscles of the perineal area, or pelvic floor, in
preparation for the trauma of childbirth. The women are in-
structed to sit on the floor, legs crossed, and gradually contract,
then slowly relax, these muscles. You would think this would be
fairly intimate activity, but the instructor and the women all seem
very nonchalant about the whole thing and are apparently un-
aware that the males in the room may be uneasy. They might be
more cognizant of the awkwardness of the situation if they had to
share a room with a dozen or so men, all of whom were directed to
have thirty-second erections. In any case, when the instructor
says, "Now for the Kegel exercise . . . ," you might want to head
for the water fountain.

8

Tits for Tots

The Pros and Cons of Breast-feeding

There has been a radical shift away from bottle-feeding over the past few decades. Pediatricians who thirty years ago strongly endorsed formula as the ideal food for infants are now rediscovering the virtues of the time-tested mammary gland. There are entire organizations devoted to the cause of breast-feeding, notably La Leche League, Tits for Tots, and the American Society of Wet Nurses. Certainly there are undeniable advantages: breast-feeding is virtually free; there are no bottles to buy, clean or replace; and mother's milk is more easily digested and provides the baby with needed antibodies. And when the baby wakes up at 6:15 in the morning, you don't have to run to the nearest convenience store and pay $9.49 for an emergency quart of Enfamil.

Still, breast-feeding isn't for everyone, and your wife may have emotional, physical, or job-related obstacles to overcome. To find out, encourage her to fill out the following questionnaire; she should use a soft lead pencil, and the elapsed time for the test is ten minutes. Completed forms should be sent with a $20 money order to the same place in New Jersey that suckered you out of $50 in high school for scoring your SATs.

Breast-feeding Aptitude Test

1. Breast-feeding would make me feel
   (a) proud (b) maternal (c) fulfilled (d) like a cow
2. My normal bra size is
   (a) 32-A (b) 36-B (c) B-52 (d) none of your business
3. I would feel self-conscious about nursing in the presence of
   (a) a female friend (b) two female friends
   (c) a male friend (d) a mailman
4. When I think of breast-feeding, I think of
   (a) happiness (b) Nature (c) the Madonna and Child
   (d) *National Geographic* photo essays on Ethiopia
5. To "express milk" means
   (a) to squirt milk out of a breast into a bottle
   (b) to drink milk rapidly
   (c) to send milk somewhere overnight
   (d) to talk with a cow

If your wife receives a final score of 800–650, she is certainly well suited for breast-feeding. With a score of 500–650, she is less than enthusiastic, but is still a good candidate for nursing. If her score is less than 450, she should seriously consider buying formula in 50-gallon kegs.

While nursing can be a positive, even joyous experience, it can present a few aggravations that will require your understanding and support. For example, the sound of your own or *any* baby's crying can trigger a "let down" reflex that brings milk into the breasts. The result for some women can be two widening stains on either side of her blouse, which can be a real conversation-starter at social gatherings. Fortunately, leaking is easily prevented with monthly applications of DuPont's Latex Breast Caulk, available at most hardware stores for under $5.00.

If your wife is breast-feeding, she will be contacted at some point by a woman who will identify herself as a "nursing coach." Many men, upon hearing this term for the first time, understandably picture a woman wearing headphones and pacing the sidelines while she harangues her players to get out there and *suckle!* This person's motives are undoubtedly well-intentioned, but she is nonetheless a stranger, and she may irritate your wife by calling periodically to inquire about the state of her breasts. At the same time the coach will encourage your wife to attend monthly meetings in the same dank church basement where your childbirth classes were held, along with eighteen other lactating women. Should these calls become too intrusive, have your wife remind this person that while she is a nursing coach, it is a strictly titular title.

MATERNITY ⟹

9

Your Ward, and Welcome to It

Coping with the Hospital

Your wife may harbor exaggerated fears about entering the hospital. She may perceive it as a stark, forbidding building, filled with diseases of all sorts, where incompetent and uncaring medical personnel inflict terrible trauma upon trusting, innocent souls. It is your job to reassure her. Remind her that our hospitals are ranked among the best in the world, that our doctors and nurses must meet the highest professional standards before being allowed to practice medicine. Explain that while there is a small element of risk, it doesn't outweigh the enormous benefits of having available the latest in modern medical technology. Still, if it will make your wife feel more secure, buy an indelible ink pad and stamp DO NOT REMOVE on any parts of her body she's concerned about losing.

The best thing you can do for your wife is to help her master techniques for coping with the contingencies that may confront her in the hospital. For example, there is the real possibility that your wife's Ob/Gyn will not be present to deliver your baby. He may not be "on call" that day, or he may have a family emergency, or an urgent convention to attend in St. Tropez. This would leave your wife in the hands of a partner she may have met only once or twice, and with whom she has little rapport. He is invariably an old codger who wants to retire next year and who belongs to the "old" school of gynecology, which regards women as lowly, inferior creatures related to man but actually far closer to cocker spaniels. He refers to your wife as "honey," "dear," or "toots."

The solution here is to avoid this situation altogether. Pick a gynocologist who has *at least* one other partner you could be satisfied with in an emergency, and make them take a solemn oath that one or the other will be there for the delivery. If they are reluctant to take such a pledge, for only $2.00 you can order a book jacket with the title *Malpractice Made Easy!* It can be trimmed to fit over most hardcover books, and will make a useful prop at your wife's next appointment.

Another common hospital hazard is the foreign resident who may care for your wife before your Ob/Gyn arrives, as well as during those other periods he is tending to other patients. For the sake of argument, we will call him Dr. Ramiswan Bhahadish. His

education is impeccable, his medical techniques irreproachable, and he is outgoing and friendly. The fact that he is incomprehensi- ble 85 percent of the time is his only flaw. Your wife's sense of well-being will not be enhanced by his cheery greeting: "Please to excuse me, but I would need for this moment to introduce my knuckles to the cervix of your spouse." Useful interaction in the face of this handicap will be extremely difficult.

For most people, the thought of a hospital tour is only slightly more appetizing than a field trip to a penitentiary for the criminally insane. Nevertheless, you and your wife should make it a point to visit the facility where you intend to have your baby, and acquaint yourselves with the environment and personnel of the maternity ward. Most hospitals have regular tours for this purpose, and the cost is nominal: $2.00/adult, $1.00/child, and free for any couple accompanied by a fetus.

When you arrive at the hospital, drive to the visitors' parking area, but carefully note where the emergency entrance is, in case the baby decides to make a nocturnal appearance (hospitals usually close their lobby doors at 10:00 P.M. for security reasons, which ensures that any muggers, thieves, and pickpockets will have to come in with you through the emergency room doors). Parking lots at medical facilities are extremely crowded due to the reluctance of seriously ill people to use bicycles, roller skates, or motorcycles as means of transportation. Consequently, you should plan to drop your wife off at the main entrance, and walk back after parking the car; bring a good-quality pair of hiking shoes.

Once inside the lobby, make your way to the maternity ward, bearing in mind that these moments in transit are fraught with peril. Bacteria and viruses of every description are floating willy-nilly around the hospital corridors, looking for unsuspecting victims. Your best bet is to take extremely shallow breaths, look straight ahead at all times, and walk with a strong, purposeful gait; most microbes will look elsewhere if you seem to be a tough customer.

Upon reaching the maternity ward, you will be greeted by the nurse who will conduct your tour. Most likely, she will begin in one of the labor rooms, where the woman who is approaching delivery can be supervised and coached as her contractions gather in intensity and frequency. You and your wife can expect to spend hours and hours in this small, bare room with an excellent view of the back of an air conditioning vent, encrusted with three generations' worth of pigeon droppings.

The nurse will then turn to the next order of business, the fetal monitor (see drawing). This device has become standard equipment in maternity wards across the country. It simultaneously monitors uterine contractions and the baby's heartbeat. The machine's sensors are placed on the woman's stomach, which has been smeared with a disgusting gelatinous goop that helps conduct sound and muscle impulses through the skin. To add insult to injury, these sensors are held in place either by an uncomfortable belt or by ludicrous pantaloons made of cheesecloth or recycled newspaper.

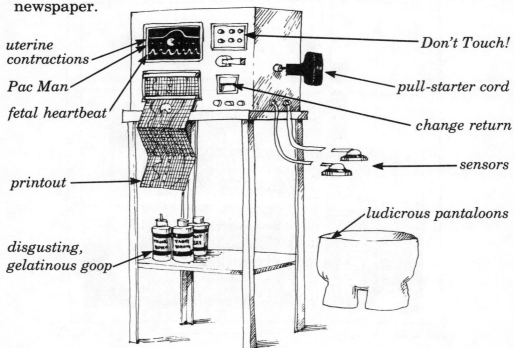

uterine contractions

Pac Man

fetal heartbeat

printout

disgusting, gelatinous goop

Don't Touch!

pull-starter cord

change return

sensors

ludicrous pantaloons

The three of you will then move on to one of the delivery rooms. These rooms are equipped to handle not only vaginal but cesarian births, should the latter prove necessary. (In all respects, this is an operating room, and everything is spotlessly sterile. As such, it gives you a good opportunity to resume normal breathing before you move back into the general hospital atmosphere.) In the center of the delivery room is, of course, the delivery table. It closely resembles an examination table in an Ob/Gyn office, except that it comes with attractive leather arm restraints that are available in navy, black, cordovan, or taupe.

A final option, frequently available, is the "birthing room," which represents an attempt to replace the stark, sterile quality that characterizes the maternity room environment. The birthing room establishes a friendly, relaxed, home-like atmosphere through the addition of throw rugs, paintings, and living room furniture, with adjoining areas for a sauna, wet bar, jogging track, complete Nautilus gym, Jacuzzi, and an espresso machine.

While the nurse is explaining some of the hospital procedures and regulations, you may hear moaning, whimpering, howling, and sporadic wailing. You will be unaccustomed to this unless of course you are an auditor for the Internal Revenue Service. The two of you should try as much as possible to take this in stride.

If your maternity ward doesn't have these items, talk to the hospital administration. They are always open to constructive suggestions.

10

The Pregnant Pause

The Ninth Month

The ninth month of pregnancy is one of Nature's favorite practical jokes (belly-button lint is another). It is filled with so much physical discomfort and emotional trauma that the Marquis de Sade would have happily claimed credit for it if he could. A complete list of the tribulations associated with this period would take up ten entire pages, even using the teeny-weeny little letters they use for insurance policies. Consequently, only a few of the most common problems can be covered here.

Braxton-Hicks contractions: Many women suffer from these unexpected, sporadic contractions, named after the two physicians who first studied this phenomenon. (Doctors love to have their names forever associated with things like unpleasant muscle spasms or sexual organs that face the wrong direction.) Your wife, besides suffering from the pain itself, may be embarrassed about suddenly doubling over in a restaurant, library, or movie theater. The best thing you can do is act as though nothing unusual is occurring. If necessary, bend down next to her and pretend to look for a lost contact lens; unfortunately, this ploy wears a little thin after the third episode in less than an hour.

Getting dressed: This simple act becomes quite complicated for a fully pregnant woman, and your wife may need your assistance with any button, latch, or zipper not directly beneath her chin. This is especially true of dress or snow boots; left to her own devices, your wife will probably spend an exasperating hour rolling around the floor like a turtle with hemorrhoids.

Mail: The charge slips you innocently signed in baby stores now come back to haunt you in the form of unsolicited baby magazines, life insurance pitches, and (heaven help you!) catalogues. Almost overnight, your home will be inundated with these glossy brochures from mail order establishments, all peddling items such as sterling silver nipple brushes, designer diaper pails, and goat's-milk teething biscuits imported from Switzerland. Once they begin to arrive, you are trapped. These catalogues will continue to appear three times a year until either you order something or your wife undergoes menopause, whichever comes first.

Entertainment: Finding diversions to ease the tensions of this final month presents a particularly thorny problem. Many couples find themselves repeatedly engaging in the following sort of conversation:

Husband: "Say, honey, why don't we get out of here this afternoon?"

Wife: "Great! How?"

Husband: "Why don't we go take in a movie?"

Wife: "How can I enjoy a movie when I have to pee every twenty minutes?"

Husband: "How about lunch at a restaurant?"

Wife: "I'm already fifteen pounds over what I'm supposed to weigh."

Husband: "Then how about going to the art museum?"

Wife: "Walking makes my feet swell up."

Husband: "Well, dammit, then how about a quick drink in a bar?"

Wife:	"You know I can't drink while I'm pregnant."
50 Husband:	"Well . . . then I guess it's another session of 'Funny Telephone Book Names.' What're we up to?"
Wife:	"Let's see . . . page 1894 . . . Glotznacker, Raphael B."

Exercise: This is a marvelous activity for your wife, and there is absolutely no reason why she can't continue to pursue a sport such as tennis. Of course, her backhand, serve, overhead, half-volley, and approach shots will all be badly hampered, and her net game all but nonexistent; still, there is a lot your wife can do if she can be consistent, pick her passing shots carefully, and hit a forehand like Ivan Lendl.

Swimming is another popular option among women in the later stages of pregnancy, and it unquestionably provides wonderful conditioning. Ocean swimming should probably be avoided, and pregnant women should take particular care not to sunbathe together. In groups of more than two, they tend to resemble schools of beached whales, and there is the ever-present risk of being dragged out to sea by overzealous marine biologists.

Overdue Pregnancy: There are a considerable number of couples who will have to endure the terrible strains of this situation. They are easy to spot, with their characteristically glazed expressions, disheveled hair and clothing, and unintelligible speech patterns. They are often picked up by authorities as vagrants or "bag couples."

If your wife is overdue by more than four days, suggest to her the following measures to bring on the onset of labor: jumping

rope, riding in a 1967 VW with worn shocks, wearing high heels on the wrong feet for an hour a day, and rubbing her breasts with tofu. None of these things will help in the least, but they should help keep her preoccupied.

If you should come across a labor-inducing method that does work, send in a twenty-five word description of the technique, fifty cents, and two box tops to "Prompt Birth Contest," % the publisher of this book. All entries must be in by July 20 and all judges' decisions are final.

11

Ready or Not

Labor and Delivery

All right. This is it. After nine and a half tiring months, your wife awakens you from a sound sleep and says, "I think it's time to go to the hospital." What should you do?

Stay calm! There is nothing to be gained by running around the house like a squirrel on amphetamines. While time is at a premium, there is usually ample opportunity to get to the hospital. Your first order of business should be to notify the doctor that you are on your way. Next, review the contents of your wife's hospital bag to make sure that you have included the following essential items:

- 2 nightgowns, a robe, and slippers
- 2 nursing bras (in case one of the nurses needs one)
- radio or cassette player w/headphones (Sony has just introduced its new "Birthman," with AM/FM radio, tape player, and built-in fetal monitor)
- signal flares

- birth announcements, envelopes, and stamps. Don't forget to bring along your address book with important addresses and phone numbers, 30 percent of which are by now totally obsolete; this provides your wife with hours of entertaining detective work.
- medical insurance identification cards. If you don't have medical insurance, bring jewelry, deeds to any property you may own, the family silver, etc.

As a final precaution, let the dog out. There is nothing worse than coming home after an exhausting birth to find a baby gift from Shep on your living room carpet.

Contrary to the stereotype of the husband speeding his wife to the hospital, you should drive with the utmost care. This is not the time to disregard the rules of the road, unless you find yourself behind a cigar-smoking boob in a fire-engine red Cadillac. Should this be the case, give him seven or eight long blasts of your horn, tailgate extremely closely, and speed past him at the first available moment, displaying the middle digit of your right hand and glaring angrily as you do so. Having successfully completed the maneuver, shrink down into your seat when your wife remarks that she's pretty sure that was her obstetrician.

Once in the maternity ward, help your wife get settled into one of the labor rooms. She should undress quickly, slip into a hospital gown, and practice her breathing techniques while she waits for a nurse to hook her up to the fetal monitor. At this point your wife's contractions may stop entirely. This tends to occur during the initial, or "prodromal," stage of birth (a term derived from the Greek

myth of Prodromia, an unpleasant maiden who made a rude re-
mark to Zeus and was sentenced to spend the rest of eternity in
the early stages of labor).

ADMISSIONS

If the staff confirms that labor has genuinely begun, you will
have to register your wife as an in-patient. This is one of Nature's
immutable laws: women have babies, and men have to deal with
ladies behind hospital admissions desks. After an interminable
wait, your number is finally called. You sit down in a cramped,
cheerless cubicle, and there she is—Ermaline Ferndissel. A dour

woman of about sixty, she apparently purchases her clothes at a thrift shop in the Twilight Zone, and has not appreciably changed her coiffure since the Dorsey Brothers played together. She will request the following information about your wife: Social Security number, date of birth, religion, hobbies, unusual sexual habits, and who she voted for in the last presidential election. Answer these questions quickly and cheerfully; Ms. Ferndissel has ways of making you talk.

This chore completed, you will return immediately to the labor room, where a resident has just finished examining your wife. To your surprise, Dr. Bhahadish is off today. His replacement is an eager but equally incomprehensible Brazilian. From the three fingers he keeps waving in the air, it is safe to assume that your wife should deliver in about three hours, unless it means that she is going to have triplets.

Assuming that your wife is handling her contractions well and is still in early labor, go change into the delivery room garb. This opportunity to see the inside of an actual doctors' lounge can be a real treat. Here it all is! The sofa where they crash during those debilitating thirty-eight-hour shifts, the lockers where they exchange their civilian clothes for the exalted vestments of Healers. Get dressed quickly. You will find at the bottom of the locker a box of shriveled rags with elasticized openings. They slip over your shoes; this information should save you about fifteen minutes of trying them out as surgical earmuffs, mittens, or as sanitary change purses for holding your germ-ridden coins and bills.

Returning to the labor room, you will find your wife's obstetrician apologizing for being late. Some moron ran him off the road, and it took him half an hour to get towed out of a ditch. He scrutinizes the printout from the fetal monitor and carefully checks your wife, waiting patiently for the peak of a painful contraction to give her an internal examination; this is necessary to gauge the dilation of the cervix. If your wife is more than 6 centimeters dilated, he will probably recommend that she move to the delivery table. Wait for the contraction to end, then help her waddle across the hall, doing a fair imitation of a three-legged watermelon race in the process.

Once on the table, let your wife establish a position that is comfortable for *her*. She is not obliged to use the stirrups just because they are there. In fact, there are literally dozens of positions that are now considered acceptable. Here are just a few:

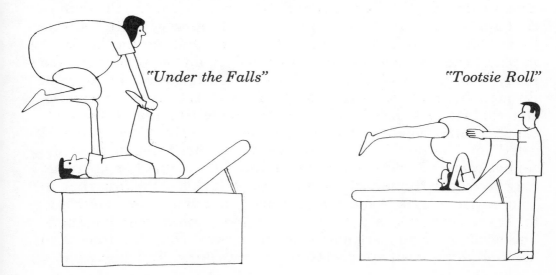

"Under the Falls"

"Tootsie Roll"

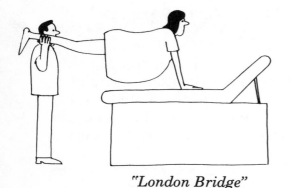

"London Bridge"

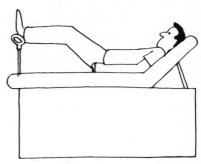

"Here, you do it."

As the cervix widens, the pace of labor may quicken. If it has not done so already, the "bag of water" will break, allowing the amniotic fluid to spill out, along with two dozen grocery store coupons that expired months ago. By now the doctor and nurses should be in place, the baby's warming bed turned on, and equipment at the ready. As your wife dilates to 8–10 centimeters, she will go through the most agonizing stage of labor, the transition phase. Her contractions may be almost unbearable (the reason they are called contractions is that women often scream things like "I can't!" or "I won't!"). She may believe at this moment that she cannot continue without the use of anesthetics, and her language may become extremely abusive. Ignore it. If this is the first time in your entire marriage she has suggested that you have a meaningful sexual experience with your own body, count your blessings. She needs your support now more than ever. Help her to control her breathing, switching patterns if necessary. Tell her what a

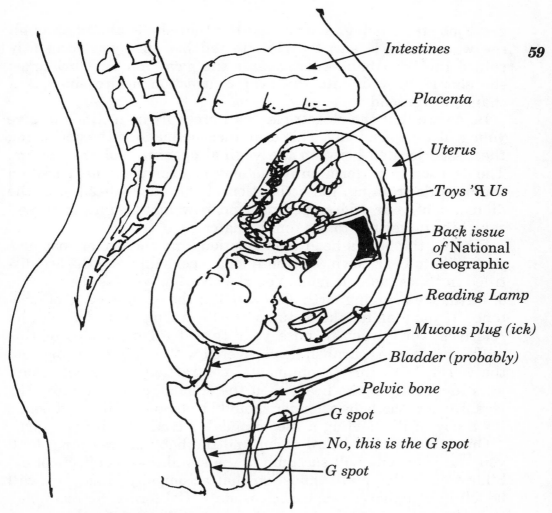

59

Intestines

Placenta

Uterus

Toys 'Я Us

Back issue of National Geographic

Reading Lamp

Mucous plug (ick)

Bladder (probably)

Pelvic bone

G spot

No, this is the G spot

G spot

Full-term Pregnancy

great job she is doing, and remind her that she is almost through the worst. This is also the time to tell her that you accidently ruined the Irish hand-knit sweater she gave you for Christmas; she should be well into the next contraction before she has a chance to respond.

Be aware that the obstetrician will probably be inclined to give your wife an episiotomy. This is an incision made in the perineum, the tissue located between the vaginal opening and the rectum. The decision to perform an episiotomy is a complex one, based on the doctor's training, his estimation of the baby's head size, the diameter of your wife's opening, and how many minutes it will save him in getting to his tennis match.

Finally, the baby's head is in position, and the doctor instructs your wife to bear down. All those long weeks and months are distilled in this single moment. You are about to witness the miracle of birth, the bringing forth of new life in the endless cycle of existence. If you plan to take pictures, start snapping; your friends and relatives won't want to miss your three-by-five glossies of this puffy, misshapen, purplish head covered with muck emerging into the world. With three monumental contractions, your wife manages to clear first the head, then the shoulders, and, finally, the legs. By now the baby's gender should be obvious: if it has a penis, it's a boy; if it's holding a Bloomingdale's credit card, it's a girl.

Once the umbilical cord is cut and the baby is breathing, both you and your wife will succumb to the simultaneous effects of exhilaration, relief, and exhaustion that accompany birth. You will be left in a euphoric, semiconscious state (California, for example). It is through this excited haze that you will watch as the nurses clean off and footprint the baby, and the doctor delivers the placenta and makes any necessary sutures.

If your wife requests it, she can hold the baby for a few minutes before he or she is carted off to the nursery. This allows for a "bonding period," the importance of which cannot be overstated. Babies deprived of this experience turn into individuals who have difficulty maintaining love relationships, have troubled marriages, and move their lips when they read. (Aha! I saw you!)

You should certainly take this opportunity to hold the baby too. It is one of life's most magnificent sensations. It will be hard for you to believe that this tentative, squirming ball of flesh will eventually walk, talk, go to malls, drive, leave home, and cost you a quarter of a million dollars in the bargain.

12

Stork Reality

Back in the Room

After the ordeal of delivery, your wife will be physically and emotionally drained. During her three- or four-day hospital recuperation, it will be your responsibility to make the final preparations for the baby's arrival. This should include giving the nursery a thorough cleaning, placing a plastic liner bag in the diaper pail, and stocking the changing table with baby wipes, lotion, and powder. Finally, you must make sure the crib is ready for the baby. Getting a fitted sheet onto a crib mattress is analogous to placing a peeled onion at the bottom of a tall glass and then trying to put the skin back on. Unfortunately, there are no easy answers, no handy little tricks to lessen the ordeal; each man must find his own answer. Chances are that if you finish the job with two dislocated thumbs and a fractured finger, you've done it properly.

Your wife's spirits will be immeasurably lifted if you send her a token of your love after the birth of the baby. Should you be unable to devise a personalized note or gift, flowers or baskets of fruit will suffice. At all costs, avoid singing telegrams. Just as your wife has found a pause in the busy hospital routine for a desperately needed nap, an unemployed actress dressed as a bellhop bursts in doing a convincing Merman-esque rendition of "Happy Birthday." This wakes not only your wife, but her roommate, the rest of the maternity ward, and three patients undergoing surgery two floors below.

Like every new parent, you will naturally experience a special thrill when the shade of the nursery window is raised and your baby is placed in view alongside the motley collection of other new arrivals. Each of your visitors should dutifully engage in a discussion of the minutest details of the baby's features: the delicacy of the fingers, the prominence of the forehead, the easily discerned intelligence in his eyes, and the lusty, vibrant quality of his wailing. Unfortunately, there is the occasional friend or relative who is too simple-minded to pick up on these traits that are so obvious to everyone else. For them, careful study of the following drawings may be necessary.

Your baby   *Another baby*

In many institutions, one item has improved noticeably in recent years: the food. Hospital fare was once considered identical to that provided by the army, only somewhat cleaner. The portions are now reasonably tasty and so generous that many women are unable to finish them. The husbands gratefully devour the remnants as a supplement to their meager diet of peanut butter and jelly sandwiches. If propriety demands it, smuggle the items out for ravaging at a later time.

This "nouvelle cuisine d'hospital" culminates in the candlelight dinner the evening prior to your wife's departure. Held in the prestigious "Top o' the Ward" staff lounge, it is elegant dining at its best. You will be surrounded by lush ferns and exotic flowers hanging from rustic stainless steel IV hooks. Soft music from vintage speakers sets a romantic mood, interspersed with dozens of intriguing urgent announcements to the medical staff. Specialties of the house include Shrimp Temperatura, Veal Scalpelini, and Lobster Newburg served over an adjustable bed of rice. Dress is semiformal: for the men, a sport coat and tie are required; for the ladies, a formal terrycloth bathrobe and appropriate slippers (nothing with bunny ears, please!). And the price? All of this is included *free of charge* with your $350-per-day-room.

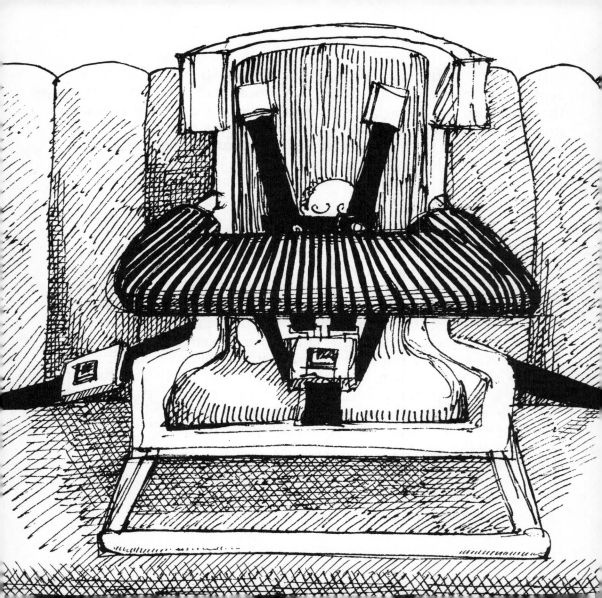

13

Home Again, Home Again, Jig-a-dee Jig

Returning from the Hospital

It's hard to believe, but the day will finally arrive when you bring the baby home from the hospital. While this is an auspicious and thrilling occasion, there are a number of associated complications for which you should be prepared.

The first of these is the carseat, or "passive child restraint" (if you are one of the lucky couples who have a passive child, you should be in good shape). It is both illegal and dangerous to travel with passengers under age three unless they are buckled into one of these devices. Any good-quality carseat should be able to withstand the impact of a grand piano dropped from a fourth-story window. It should come equipped with a rear strap that can be bolted to the chassis of the car; most mechanics will do this for under $50, or you can do it yourself and drill a hole in your gas tank.

Most often the initiation of the carseat takes place on the way home from the hospital. There is inevitably a long line of cars behind you waiting their turn to pick up incapacitated relatives at the entrance. Although you may have reviewed the directions several times, you will be hopelessly bewildered by this infuriating contraption. The honking behind you will reach a sustained, fevered pitch. When you finally achieve success, the spectacle of your newborn snared in this web of straps, buckles, snaps, and bars is so pathetic that you unshackle him immediately. Your wife carries the baby on her lap as you drive homeward, feeling terribly guilty and apprehensive.

By the time you arrive home, your household should be in the capable hands of visiting mothers or mothers-in-law who have "come to help out." While their intentions are the very best, "new" grandmothers can often create more difficulties than they solve. They generally fall into one of two categories. The first doesn't actually *do* anything, but chooses to offer frequent bits of unsolicited advice, such as, "Aren't you supposed to hold the baby more upright?" or, "Don't you wipe the baby's crib with Lysol once a day?" More insidious is the willing assistant who insists that your wife lie down and let *her* do it. Say, for example, that she has elected to help straighten the kitchen. After one minute on the job, the following exchange begins, with your wife having to holler at the top of her lungs to make herself heard from her bedroom.

Mother: "Beverly!"
Wife: "What?"
Mother: "Where's the floor wax?"
Wife: "The Borax?"
Mother: *"No, the floor wax!"*
Wife: *"It's under the sink!!"*
Mother: "Well, I can't find it!!"

This, of course, means that your wife is forced to drag herself out of bed to locate the elusive floor wax. This performance is repeated almost verbatim for the vacuum cleaner, the laundry detergent, the baby's undershirt, spaghetti sauce for dinner, and hair spray, which your wife has not used since her prom night. As with other delicate family matters, accept this situation with quiet good humor, and wait until Mother leaves to have an all-out marital dogfight with your spouse.

With Mother's departure, however, comes the awesome realization that you are now solely reponsible for the well-being of a totally helpless infant. This sensation becomes most acute whenever the baby cries, creating a mild form of uncontrollable panic. Your natural instinct will be to prod your wife into continuously nursing the baby, even though he may have eaten beautifully only a half hour before. Resist the temptation. Instead, you could walk or rock the baby, make sure his diaper is clean, sing songs to him, or try giving him a bath. Then if all else fails, say nothing but give your wife a stare that subtly accuses her of being an unfit mother. This may work several times before you end up in another all-out marital dogfight.

On the first occasion the baby spits up, your sense of desperation can be profound; you may actually imagine your baby losing weight even as you change his soiled stretchsuit. Fortunately, these fears pass away as the baby establishes his normal eating patterns. After a few short months you will be amazed at how blasé you will be about regurgitated milk. Many fathers find that they can successfully continue eating dinner, wiping the baby's gastric offerings with one hand and taking second helpings of beef stew with the other.

Finally, there is the problem of the "postpartum blues." This is a severe depression brought on by hormonal fluctuations occurring after birth, made worse by the difficulties of meeting the new baby's continual demands. Uncontrollable weeping, withdrawal, or unexplained, irrational displays of anger are common symptoms. And to make matters worse, your wife may suffer from these too.

14

Winning the Poo

The Diaper Dilemma

Many baby books don't have the courage to deal with this difficult subject. Either the authors are too squeamish or they are afraid of offending their readers, which obviously isn't an issue if you've made it this far in the book. Nevertheless, the problem of dealing with your baby's excrement is a serious one that deserves to be treated in an intelligent, adult manner, without resorting to crude scatological references, childish double entendres, and tasteless puns like the one at the top of the page.

You and your wife will have to decide whether to use cloth or paper diapers; like anything else, there are pluses and minuses to either option. Cloth diapers are less convenient and require great manual dexterity, cumbersome pins, irritating plastic pants, and thorough cleaning when they become soiled. On the other hand, cloth diapers are much cheaper, and have the added advantage of being serviceable after the baby no longer needs them. Old diapers can be made into bedspreads, placemats, drapes, and commemorative flags.

Paper diapers are unquestionably more expensive, but they are much easier to use and are virtually foolproof. The only possible mistake you can make is to inadvertently transfer baby powder from your hands onto the diaper tapes, rendering one or both entirely useless. At that point, you have only two options: (1) throw out a perfectly good diaper, or (2) run around the house with a squirming baby, trying on tape, twine, clamps, and finally self-hardening epoxy; *then* throw out the diaper, which is no longer perfectly good.

The only other argument against paper diapers is the ecological one. Every baby who uses them exclusively wears the equivalent of three good-sized elm trees before he's potty-trained. Surprisingly, many couples who have concurrent memberships in the Sierra Club, the Cousteau Society, and the American Wildlife Federation don't even flinch at the prospect of defoliating the earth so long as they don't have to wash their kid's doody balls in the toilet.

Finally, there is the problem of disposing of paper diapers while away from home. There is an almost irresistible temptation to simply toss the offending item into the nearest open receptacle. This may be acceptable at a playground, perhaps, but is decidedly unacceptable at a restaurant, place of worship, or your mother-in-law's house. Say, for example, that you and your wife are in a fast-food establishment with your baby, and little Sheila has come up with one more McNugget than you bargained for. What do you do? You can't leave the diaper on a tray with a note that says, "Have it *our* way." The wisest approach is to insert it into an empty soda cup or french fry container and nonchalantly throw it into the trash bin on your way out. The only other option is to take the offending

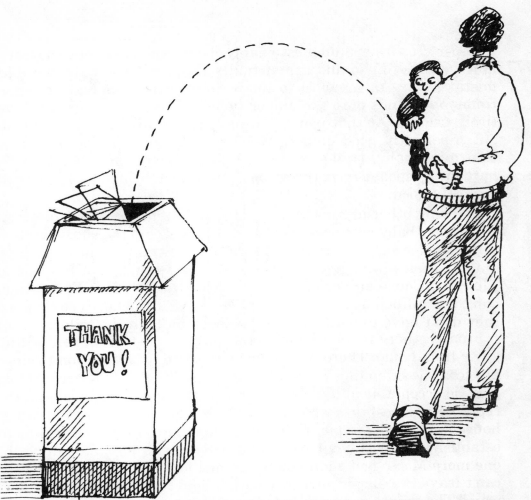

diaper home with you; you run the risk, however, of having it roll under the seat, only to be discovered after the interior of your car has to be removed and sent to the dry cleaners for fumigation.

15

Oh God! The Baby's Up

Late-Night Feedings

Young men who became fathers even a decade ago were generally exempted from administering late-night feedings. They, after all, were obliged to arise early every morning and, except for sporadically held board meetings, had little opportunity to catch up on lost sleep. Now, what with child-rearing and housekeeping acknowledged to be demanding responsibilities, and increasing numbers of women either choosing or being forced to enter the work market, many men are now sharing in the joys of the 3:00 A.M. bottle. Even when the wife has elected to breast-feed, the liberated husband is eager to participate by changing the baby and offering companionship to his nursing wife.

This is new territory for men generally and for new fathers in particular, so a typical evening is depicted here for the benefit of the uninitiated.

You are in the middle of an extremely satisfying dream somehow involving Linda Ronstadt, a Lucite pepper mill, and three

quarts of 10-40 motor oil. A plaintive wail pierces your sleep-soaked mind like an artillery shell through Kleenex, and your eyes spring open, staring into darkness, searching for a reason for this cruel interruption. The cry is repeated, this time in earnest.

Your wife rustles beneath the bedcovers, and identifies the offending sound. "Alan, the baby. . . . Alan, *the baby!!*"

You stabilize your pupils long enough to read the digital clock on the night table: 4:25 A.M. You throw off the blanket and, in a monumental effort of will, activate enough of your cerebral cortex to follow the noise to its source. Half-stumbling into the nursery, you flick on the light, and there, grinning wildly, is your baby, lying in a nightie saturated with all manner and kinds of excrement. You are spared from gagging only because that reflex hasn't managed to get out of bed yet. The mopping-up operation accomplished, you carry your bundle of joy back to your bedroom where your wife, in the soft glow of some obscure lamp, lies with her breasts exposed like a Madonna by Raphael. She begins nursing the baby while you, with faint hope, turn on the television: this is not in the expectation of entertainment per se, but simply to have a moving image to focus upon. You settle upon the final half of a Canadian horror film, *Maniacs from Manitoba*. The baby is fed, burped, and back to sleep within twenty minutes. To your undying embarrassment and shame, you stay up another half hour to watch the end of the movie.

16

The Longest Mile

Traveling with the Baby

No shock will come quite so rudely as the logistical difficulties of getting around with the baby. A few months ago the two of you could have thrown a sleeping bag into the car at a moment's notice and headed off to the mountains for a quiet weekend alone. With the baby, that same weekend will now be neither quiet nor alone, and will require more equipment than a lunar landing.

Many couples are confused about what items are essential to bring for an overnight stay with the baby. You should be able to survive brief periods with a portable crib (with sheets), a carton of diapers, changes of baby clothes, a pacifier, baby wipes, spit-up cloths, and formula with bottles and nipples if your wife is not nursing. Many parents also bring along a canvas baby carrier, a variation of the old Indian "papoose" that allows you mobility while having easy access to the baby. These can be worn either on your stomach or back with a readjustment of the straps; be forewarned, however, that such alterations require ingenuity, dexterity, and perseverance. Most users generally surrender when one strap has cut off their air supply, the other strap has a stranglehold on their groin, and the baby is dangling somewhere below their knees.

Packing the car for extended vacations can become a particularly grueling ordeal. In addition to the items listed above, you must make room for all your own luggage and recreational gear. Fortunately, there are some tricks that can help. You can save valuable space by packing the diapers in small recesses around the car such as the glove compartment, under the seats, or in those wasted areas around the engine block. If you are bringing a stroller or portable crib with wheels, tie it to the back bumper and let it roll behind the car. Finally, if you have a roof rack or can rent one, pack as much as you can on top of the car without buckling the metal. When you have an arrangement that seems satisfactory, cover it with a waterproof vinyl sheet and secure it tightly with a heavy nylon rope. Properly executed, you should be able to drive for ten to fifteen minutes before the tarp comes undone and begins to flap around the car so maddeningly that you are forced to stop and rip the thing to shreds, resulting in a $50 fine for littering.

The highlight of your trip comes just as a torrential rainstorm has forced you to close all the windows and slow down to a crawl. You become aware at this precise moment that the baby has made a substantial deposit in his diaper that demands immediate attention. Pull over to the shoulder and stop beneath the first available underpass. Step out of the car, sinking your left foot ankle-deep into a water-filled pothole. Open the door adjacent to the baby, unbuckle him, and lay him down on the back seat. Try to ignore the tractor-trailers that thunder by the car, missing it by mere inches and spraying you with a viscous soup made from rainwater, oil, dirt, and rubber. Get the diaper undone and swear bitterly when you realize that it's perfectly clean. Reassemble the baby, put him back in his seat, get back in the car, and drive on in sullen silence. After ten minutes, accuse your wife of having farted and not owning up to it.

The two of you must endure one final trial: your baby, no matter how good-natured, will begin screaming shortly before you reach your destination. Nothing you do will make the slightest difference. Pacifiers, toys, rattles, bottles of juice, making funny faces, and playing the radio all fail one by one. Junior will continue to increase the decibel level with every passing minute, until at last the rear view mirror shatters and rivets start popping out of the chassis. This is the time to make the most of that portable crib rolling behind the car. You won't hear a thing once you're over 35 miles per hour.

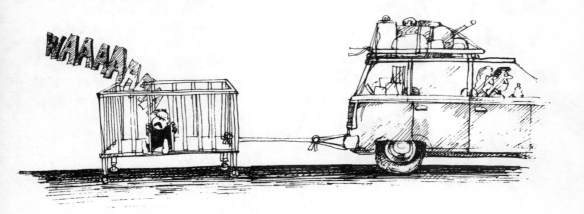

17

The Great Escape

The First Night Out

The day will eventually come when you and your wife decide that you simply have to get out of the house for an adult evening, without a baby seat in your right hand, a diaper bag in your left, and a pacifier hidden in your breast pocket. You decide to throw caution to the wind and make a reservation at a pricey French restaurant, and for a moment you believe your weekend plans are settled. They are not.

For beginning on this day, and for the next twelve years of your life, your leisure arrangements will have to include the quest for The Baby-Sitter. Finding prepubescent girls will become a major obsession for you and your wife. You ask your friends with children if they know of any kids who sit; even if they do, they're likely to keep her a secret, as a good sitter ranks well above South African Krugerrands in the young parents' set of priorities. You find yourself haunting malls and video game arcades in the hope of spotting a likely prospect, but to no avail. Finally, you receive a hot tip from a secretary at work who has a cousin whose girlfriend baby-sits. She lives two counties away, but your situation is becoming more desperate with every passing hour. You call her up but are intercepted by the girl's mother, who demands the number of your driver's license, two credit cards, and three character references. Satisfied that you are probably not a raving sexual psychopath, she puts her daughter on, and you make the necessary arrangements.

The hours prior to your departure are frantic. The baby must be washed, changed, fed, and put to sleep. As the baby may wake up hungry, your wife, if she's a purist about breast-feeding, must express her milk into a bottle. After a half hour's squeezing, her breasts are thoroughly raw and there is an ounce of milk to show for her efforts. Deciding that she is no longer a purist, she makes a bottle of formula.

On your way to pick up the sitter, you become utterly lost because you miss several key street signs in the dark. You obtain directions in an all-night gas station with a gargantuan Doberman who shows extreme interest in your left leg. Thirty minutes late, you finally arrive at the girl's home.

You beep your horn, and the sitter, Lolita Ripley, trots out to your car, several textbooks in her arms. Many men are astonished to find that despite their years of hard-won experience and expanded vistas, they are not appreciably better at conversing with cute thirteen-year-old girls than they were at thirteen. After exhausting the subjects of her grade level, favorite subject, the clubs she belongs to, and how many siblings she has, you lapse into an interminable and painful silence.

Upon arriving back home, you find your wife struggling to get dressed while tending to an extremely unhappy child, who no doubt senses the conspiracy that's afoot. You take the bawling baby in your arms, which is the signal for him to send gobbets of spit-up dribbling down your best wool blazer. For most couples, this is the breaking point. Your wife laterals the baby to the sitter, you wish her all the luck in the world, and you both do wind sprints out to the car. You tear off into the night, leaving behind a lingering cloud of rubber and exhaust.

This is it, your first evening out alone with your wife in over ninety long days. There are no diapers at Henri's, no pacifiers to search for behind sofas, no booties to slip onto squirming feet. And the entire time, through your Chianti, the stuffed mushrooms, the veal piccata and boeuf bourguignon, the only thing the two of you can talk about is whether the baby is all right.